T0134803

Reagan the Penguin Plays Hockey

Written and Illustrated by
Michelle LeMaster

AuthorHouse™
1663 Liberty Drive
Bloomington, IN 47403
www.authorhouse.com
Phone: 1 (800) 839-8640

Published by AuthorHouse 09/24/2018

ISBN: 978-1-5462-5897-1 (sc)
ISBN: 978-1-5462-5898-8 (e)

Print information available on the last page.

This book is printed on acid-free paper.

authorHOUSE®

Dedication

Dedicated to my nephew! Never give in to the dream-killers because they are fearful of dreams out of reach. Dream big little one!

Playing hockey was one of Reagan the Penguin's biggest dreams.

Reagan dreamed of playing hockey with the bigger penguins. He wanted to play hockey just like his daddy. His daddy was one of the best hockey players in the waddle and taught Reagan how to play hockey. With the help of Frankie, Reagan was unstoppable… except the bigger penguins would not let him play.

But Reagan could zoom across ice.
He zig-zagged between penguins and
they didn't even notice. His small
size made him invisible. Frankie
was smart and always gave Reagan
tips on skating and playing hockey.
But the bigger penguins would not
give either of them a chance because
they were different!

Reagan was much shorter and smaller than the other penguins in the waddle. He was on the team but never got to play. Frankie was made fun of because he was so much smarter than the other teammates. They called Frankie and Reagan names!

The bigger penguins made fun of his small size and his big dreams. They laughed and teased "You're too little! You can't swim or skate as fast as us! You'd be a better shrimp! You can't have big dreams and you can't play hockey!"

Reagan slumped and whimpered to himself, "Maybe they are right! I am tiny. But I'm good at hockey! Oh, I'll never get a chance!" he groaned throwing his flippers in the air.

"Don't listen to them Reagan!" Frankie urged, "You can do anything you want! The only penguin stopping you is you. You're the bravest penguin with the biggest heart! We practice every morning. You are so talented!" Frankie told his best friend.

Frankie knew Reagan could do big things in the world. But he knew if the team never gave Reagan a chance, he might stop playing! *We have to stay positive,* Frankie thought, pushing his glasses back on his face.

Frankie and Reagan raced behind the bigger penguins to the ice rink to watch their teammates play the semifinal hockey game. The crowd filled the snow arena!

The crowd roared with excitement as the penguins slid out on the ice. The two teams were rivals and everybody wanted their cheers to be heard!

Reagan and Frankie jumped on the team bench waving their blue flags. "GO BOOMERANGS!" They cheered for their team! A sea of blue Boomerangs and red Racer flags waved around the ice.

Reagan imagined he was skating to the cheers. He and Frankie practiced on their own. Frankie was a good coach and Reagan was a great player.

CLINK-CLANK! The puck dropped on the ice and the sound rang into the crowd.

A Boomerang stole the puck and raced to the goal. The crowd roared as the team captain, Ricky, launched through the red wall of Racers and shot the puck!

"GOOOOAAAAAAAALLLLLL" The crowd roared. The teams battled back and forth. Frankie and Reagan didn't blink! The called plays to their team.

The game was exciting but the Racers were a good team. The crowd got nervous! The score was Boomerangs 1 – Racers 3!

"AGGGHHHH! The Racers are winning!" Frankie groaned!
Their coach shouted, demanding the team stop messing around.

Ricky took things into his own hands and as his opponent shot the puck, Ricky stole it and zoomed straight to the other goal. But a Racer came out of nowhere and swept the puck from Ricky's side and tripped him. The crowd was outraged!

"AHHHHHHHH" Ricky screamed as he flipped to his belly and slid hard into the ice bank. *CRACK!* The blade of his skate snapped in half! The horn sounded as the red team scored a goal, deflating the stands.

Everyone stopped when they heard cries of pain. The coach rushed to help Ricky. Ricky's skate was broken and his flipper was cut!

"What are we going to do?!" The team anxiously chirped, "Ricky is the best player. We can't play without him! We will never win!"

"I'll play! I can do it! Just give me a chance." Reagan pleaded and leaped to his skates, hockey stick in hand, ready to carry his team to victory.

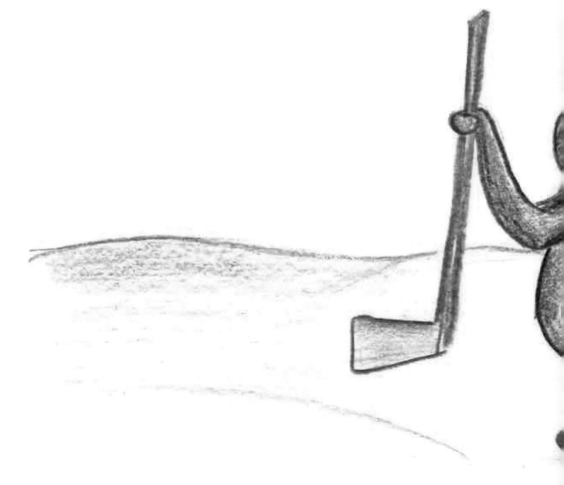

"Hahaha," the team laughed with pity, "You can't play Reagan! You're so small the Racer's will crush you! You wouldn't stand a chance!"

26

"I can do this! I can do ANYTHING!" Reagan bellowed back, "I practice so much and I practice with my dad! He taught me everything I know about hockey. Give me a chance! Please!"

The team turned away and ignored his pleas. But Reagan was determined and Frankie whispered again, "Reagan, just do it! Get on the ice and start skating!" Before Frankie finished talking, Reagan leapt over the ice wall and onto the rink. He zipped by the other team and zig-zagged in and out of imaginary players faster than anyone had ever seen. His teammates watched in awe and surprise. They began to whisper to each other.

"Coach…" Ricky whimpered through the pain. The teammates and coach were not paying attention to Ricky, still trying to make a decision. "COACH!" He yelled, "Put Reagan in. We don't have another choice. Give him a chance. I think we need him…" Ricky sounded sheepish, feeling guilty for how he treated Reagan before without giving Reagan a chance.

The team agreed and jumped on the ice. Reagan stole the puck right away and slid between the Racers. He scored one goal. Two Goals! Three Goals! The crowd went crazy. The score was tied and the Boomerangs could go to the championship game!

There were 3 seconds left in the game. Reagan was skating hard down the rink towards the goal! "Shoot!!" The crowd panicked as the clocked ticked to 0:02! Reagan pulled back his stick and shot the puck like his dad and Frankie taught him. 0:01!

Puck sailing through the air, all the Racers scrambled to block but they were to slow.

Whoosh. The puck sailed into the net.

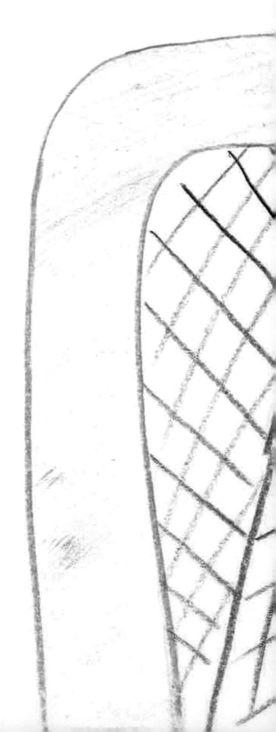

0:00 *BUZZZZZZZ!* Lights
on the scoreboard flashed
5 - Boomerangs, 4 - Racers.

The game was over! Reagan zig-zagged between players back to the bench and hugged Frankie!

"See!" Frankie chimed, "I knew you could do it. You just had to show everyone else! Maybe now they will give us a chance instead of saying no without giving us a chance!" Frankie said, bringing Reagan to the rest of his team. They hoisted Reagan over their heads chanting his name!

"We won!" the team chanted, "We won the semifinals! We are going to the championship game!"

The celebrations died down and Reagan and Frankie headed home. The team waddled up to them, "Hey! We're sorry for not giving you a chance or wanting you guys to be a part of the team. We didn't think a little penguin could play a big game." Ricky said sheepishly as the rest of the team agreed. "Reagan, I want you to play in my spot for the championship! Frankie, we need you to help create new plays! What do you think?

Reagan and Frankie looked at each other in surprise and excitedly shouted, "Yes! That'd be a dream come true!"

The penguins high-fived their teammates with a new respect *and* a new friendship! They were ready for the championship game.

Printed in the United States
By Bookmasters